From Winnie's Kitchen to Your Table

Cooking with Love

FROM WINNIE'S KITCHEN TO YOUR TABLE COOKING WITH LOVE
COPYRIGHT © 2023 BY WINNIE

SPECIAL DEDICATIONS
OF CONTRIBUTIONS

In heartfelt appreciation and acknowledgment of their
contributions to the book, I thank:

Dolly Moore Solomon

Lee Mary Sheppard

Lillie Cunningham

Brian Brenner

APPETIZERS

PAGE NO

1 • Stuffed Mushrooms — Page No 1

2 • Egg Rolls — Page No 1

3 • Taco Dip — Page No 2

4 • Sweet & Sour Meatballs — Page No 2

5 • Stuffed Zucchini — Page No 3

6 • Chili Cheese Dip — Page No 3

7 • Bean Dip — Page No 4

8 • Salmon Spread — Page No 4

9 • Lemon Butter — Page No 5

DINNER

PAGE NO

1 • Ham 'N Yam Kabobs   Page No 6

2 • Hawaiian Spareribs   Page No 6

3 • Quiche Lorraine   Page No 7

4 • Quick Chicken Broccoli Quiche   Page No 7

5 • Ten Minute Chili   Page No 8

6 • Tamale Pie   Page No 8

7 • Doritos Casserole   Page No 9

8 • Pepper Steak & Rice   Page No 9

9 • Lasagna   Page No 10

10 • Chicken Tortilla Casserole   Page No 10

11 • Pork Meatballs & Wheat Pasta   Page No 11

12 • Winnie's Drunken Turkey   Page No 11

13 • Bail Sun-Dried Tomatoes, Chicken & Pasta,or Rice   Page No 12

DINNER

PAGE NO

14 • Lemon Shrimp With Capers — Page No 12

15 • Lemon Garlic Chicken With Capers — Page No 13

16 • Chicken Pesto Cream Cheese Croissant With Sun-Dried Tomatoes — Page No 13

17 • French Onion Soup — Page No 14

18 • Turkey Stuffed Bell Pepper — Page No 14

19 • Smothered Stuffed Pork Chops — Page No 15

20 • Stuffed Cabbage — Page No 15

21 • Teriyaki Chicken With Honey Ginger Glaze — Page No 16

22 • Glaze — Page No 16

23 • Garlic Pesto Chicken — Page No 17

24 • Baked Fried Chicken — Page No 17

25 • Sprial Bourbon Glazed Ham — Page No 18

26 • Bourbon Glaze — Page No 18

27 • Catfish Nuggets — Page No 19

DESSERT

1 • Pie Crust

2 • Winnie's Fudge

3 • Lee's Apple Pie

4 • Mama's Old Fashioned Sweet Potato Pie

5 • Tripple Chocolate Pound Cake

6 • Lee Maey;s Tea Cakes

7 • Spicy Zucchini Bread

8 • Mama;s Ppecan Pie

9 • Blueberry Chocolate Chip Peanut Butter No Kaked Cookies

10 • German Chocolate Cake

11 • Coconut-Pecan Forsting

12 • Sock It To Me Cake

DESSERT

PAGE NO

13 • Banana Pudding — Page No 26

14 • Cheescake — Page No 26

15 • 7-Up Cake — Page No 27

16 • Peanut Brittle — Page No 27

17 • Tripple Chocolate Sugar-Free Cupcakes — Page No 28

18 • Apricot Fried Pies — Page No 28

19 • Peanut Butter Cranberry Cookies — Page No 29

20 • Baileys, Cinnamon French Custard Toast — Page No 29

21 • Lemon Pineapple Up-Side Down Cupcake — Page No 30

22 • Lemon Cream Cheese Pineapple Frosting — Page No 30

23 • Better Than Sex Chocolate Pie (New) — Page No 31

24 • Gingerbread (New) — Page no 31

SIDES

PAGE NO

1 • Spicy Mashed Potatoes   Page No 32

2 • Black-Eyed Peas And
Smoked Turkey   Page No 32

3 • Garlic GreenBeans With Bacon   Page No 33

4 • Nana's Southern Mac & Cheese   Page No 33

5 • Pasta Salad   Page No 34

6 • Nana's Okra And Tomatoes   Page No 34

7 • Cronbread Dressing   Page No 35

8 • Baked Beans   Page No 35

9 • ZucchiniCarrots.Broccoli
Steamed Vegrtable Salt   Page No 36

SIDES

PAGE NO

10 • Mama's Candied Yams   Page No 36

11 • Potato Salad   Page No 37

12 • Taco Salad   Page No 37

13 • Italian Chopped Salad   Page No 38

14 • Spinach Salad   Page No 38

15 • Greek Salad   Page No 39

16 • Strawberry Spinach Chicken Salad   Page No 39

17 • Garlic Roasted Potatoes   Page No 40

18 • Southern Apple Cider Vingar Cucumber Tomato & Onions   Page No 40

19 • Collard Greens   Page No 41

Appetizers

STUFFED MUSHROOMS

2   Packs of whole mushrooms
    12oz cream cheese

1   A bunch of green onion

1   Pack of bacon bits

Wash mushrooms, pull the stem, and set aside on a baking sheet. Prepare dip and microwave cream cheese for 45 seconds. Chop green onion finely. Stir cream cheese to a smooth consistency, add green onion, and add bacon bits. Stir until the mixture has an entirely creamy texture. I am using a teaspoon, scoop tsp of mix into mushrooms. Preheat oven to 350 degrees. Bake for 25 mins.

EGG ROLLS

1 1/2 lb. ground beef

One pkg. egg roll wrap

One large bell pepper, chopped.

One medium onion, chopped.

One small cabbage, chopped.

One bunch of carrots, chopped.

Cook ground beef and onion in a skillet until done drain off fat. Place bell pepper, carrots, and cabbe in hot water. Cook until tender; drain. Now put a tablespoon of meat and one tablespoon of veget in wraps and begin to wrap. (Note: Wraps have directions.) Place cooking oil in a frypan. Cook unt golden brown; drain on a paper towel.

TACO DIP

1lb Ground Meat
1 Pack taco seasoning
Can refried beans
1 ½ `lb. Velveeta Cheese Dip
1Cup chopped green onion.
18oz can of black olives

1   Chopped Tomatoes
1   Can diced Jalapenos
1/2c Chopped Red Onion
1/2c Chopped Cilantro
1c Can diced Ortega green chilies.
1/8oz can of salsa

Brown ground meat with taco seasoning. In a pot, combine refried beans with milk and chili powder for a smooth consistency. Layer half of the beans on a tray, add meat mixture, then remaining beans, and top with Velveeta cheese and desired toppings, including a dollop of sour cream if desired.

SWEET & SOUR MEATBALLS

2LB Ground Meat
1/2c Finely Chopped Onion
1/4c Finely Chopped Bell pepper
1tbs Flour
1tbs Seasoning Salt
1tbs Ground Black Pepper

2tbs Italian Breadcrumbs
1tbls Worcestershire Sauce
1tbls Worcestershire Sauce
1/2c Pineapple Juice
1/2c Barbeque Sauce
1/2c Sweet & Sour Sauce

1/3c Brown Sugar

Preheat oven to 350°F. Combine ground meat, onion, bell pepper, flour, seasoning salt, black pepper, and Italian breadcrumbs in a bowl. Form mixture into meatballs and bake on a sheet for 35 minutes. In a saucepan, mix Worcestershire sauce, ginger, pineapple juice, barbecue sauce, sweet-sour sauce, and brown sugar, bringing it to a simmer. Pour the sauce over meatballs in a crockpot and cook on low for 1½ hours.

STUFFED ZUCCHINI

6 Zucchini

1tsp Season Salt

1tsp Black Pepper

1tsp Garlic

1tsp Pesto

2tsp Lemon Juice

1/3c Feta Cheese

1/4c Parnassian Cheese

Halve and hollow out zucchini. Combine salt, pepper, garlic, pesto, lemon juice, feta cheese, and Parmesan cheese. Fill zucchini shells with the mixture. Preheat oven to 350°F and bake for 30-40 minutes until golden on top.

CHILI CHEESE DIP

1lb Ground Beef

1pkg Chili Seasoning

1 12oz Can diced tomatoes with green chili.

1 12oz Can fire roasted tomatoes.

1 ½ lb. Velveeta Cheese

15oz Can tomato sauce.

1tlbs Chili Powder

1tsb Garlic Salt

1tsb Black Pepper

1c Water

Brown ground meat, add chili packet, diced tomatoes, fire-roasted tomatoes, Tomato sauce, chili powder, and Water. Simmer for 10min. In a microwave-safe bowl, soften the cheese and fold in chili in small amounts, stirring until well mixed and served.

BEAN DIP

(8oz.) Cream Cheese

Cans Bean Dip

3 Tbsp. Hot Sauce

3 Cups Sour Cream

1 Cup Green Onions, Sliced.

2 Pkg. Taco Seasoning

1Lb Cheddar cheese (Grated)

1Lb Jack Cheese (Grated}

Beat cream cheese. Add bean dip and hot sauce, until mixed well. Add chopped green onions.
Spray the bottom of baking. dishes begin to layer the bottom of baking dish with half of bean
mixture and cover next layer with cheddar and jack cheese. Continue with next layer
with the remaining bean mixture then last layer with remaining cheese.
Bake at 325" for 25 minutes.

SALMON SPREAD

1 can Salmon

(8oz.) Cream Cheese

1 Tbsp. Lemon Juice

1 Tsp. Prepared Horseradish

2 Tsp. Grated Onion

¼ Tsp. Liquid Smoke

¼ Tsp. Salt

Mix all ingredients together refrigerate 2 hours Garnish
with fresh chopped parsley on top. Serve with a
choice of crackers.

LEMON BUTTER

½ C. Butter

3 Tbsp. lemon juice

Mix softened butter, adding lemon juice until it becomes pliable. Serve on fish.

DINNER RECIPES

HAM 'N YAM KABOBS

Two lb. Cooked Boneless Smoked Ham

(17 oz.) Can Yams

3 Tbsp. Butter or Margarine

(13 3/4 oz.) Can Pineapple
Chunks (in Pineapple Juice)

Cut yams in half, drain, and save pineapple juice. Mix 1/4 cup
pineapple juice with melted butter. Cube ham and thread it with
yams and pineapple on skewers. Broil or grill, brushing with pineapple
juice mixture, for 15-20 minutes, turning occasionally. Serves 6.

HAWAIIAN SPARERIBS

4 to 6 lb. Lean Spareribs

1/4 c. Flour

1 Tsp. Salt

1/4 c. Soy Sauce

4 Tbsp. Oil

314 c. Brown Sugar

2/3 c. Wine Vinegar

1/2 c. Water

1 (No. 2) Can Slice Pineapple

One Clove of Minced Garlic

1 Tsp. Grated Fresh Ginger.

Root or 1/2 tsp. powdered ginger

Cut spareribs into 2-inch strips. Mix fl. our, salt, and soy sauce to a smooth paste;
brush on ribs. Allow to stand for 10 minutes. Heat oil in a large skillet and
brown ribs on all sides. Transfer ribs to a large roasting pan. Pour fat
from the skillet. Add sugar, vinegar, water, pineapple juice, garlic,
and ginger. Heat and stir, loosening brown juices to pour over ribs.
Place ribs in 350" oven and bake for 1 to 1 1 /2 Hours.

QUICHE LORRAINE

/Two lb. Bacon

1/2 lb. Sliced mushrooms

1/2 lb. Sharp Cheddar Cheese, Shredded

Four Eggs, Slightly Beaten.

1 1/2 c. Milk

/2 c. Cream

1 Tsp. Salt

A Few Onions (to Taste)

1/8 Tsp. Nutmeg

1/8 Tsp. Pepper

1 (9-Inch) Unbaked Pie Shell

Bacon crisp. Sauté mushrooms in butter. Arrange both in a pie shell. Sprinkle cheese over bacon and mushrooms. Combine eggs, milk, cream, nutmeg, salt, and pepper. Blend slightly. Pour over cheese, bacon, and mushrooms. Bake at 400 ° for 30 to 40 minutes. Don't overbake. Remove while the center appears soft. Let stand for 5 to 10 minutes before serving.

QUICK CHICKEN BROCCOLI QUICHE

2 Prepared 9-Inch Deep Dish Pie Crusts

2 Large Boiled Chicken Breasts, Diced

1/2 Cup Diced Onion (regular or green)

1 Cup Raw Broccoli, Chopped into Bite-Sized Pieces

1 Cup Cheddar or Colby Cheese, Grated

1 Cup Swiss or Mozzarella Cheese, Grated

1 Cup Monterey Jack Cheese, Grated

1 1/4 Cups milk (or 3/4 Cup Milk and 3/4 Cup Chicken Broth) 5 Eggs

1 Tsp Salt

1 Tsp Pepper

1 (10 oz.) Can of Mushroom Soup

Preheat your oven to 350°F (175°C).In each pie crust, layer equally the diced chicken, diced onion, chopped broccoli, and grated cheeses, except for the mushroom soup, milk, eggs, salt, and pepper. Set aside. In a separate bowl, mix together the mushroom soup, milk, eggs, salt, and pepper. Pour the soup mixture evenly into each pie, ensuring you use the exact amount for each. Bake for 1 1/2 to 2 hours, or until a knife inserted into the middle comes out clean and the top is golden brown.

TEN MINUTE CHILI

2lb Ground Meat

McCormick Chili Packet

One Can Fire Fire-Roasted Tomatoes.

I Can Have Tomato Sauce.

One Package of Thinly Sliced Steak

One Can Dark Red Kidney Bean

One Can of Pinto Beans

3 Tablespoons Chili Powder

1 ½ Cup Water

Brown ground beef, adding seasoning, salt, black pepper, and garlic. Drain part of the excess oil from the meat, add a chili packet and the remaining ingredients, and add water to a low simmer sauté pan tsp of garlic 1/3 cup chopped onion, 2tbs of olive oil sauté the steak until done add to chill simmer for ten minutes.

TAMALE PIE

1 3/4 c. Chili Con Carne

1/2 c. Cream-style Corn

1/2 c. Chopped Green Peppers

1/2 c. Shredded Cheese

1/2 c. Sliced Ripe Olives

Corn Meal Crust:

2 1/2 c. Cold Water

1/2 Tsp. Chili Powder

1 Tsp. Salt

1 1/2 c. Yellow Cornmeal

In a saucepan, combine water, salt, chili powder, and cornmeal. Cook over medium heat for about 10 minutes until thick, stirring frequently. Reserve 3/4 cup. Butter a 1 1/2-quart casserole dish and line it with the remaining cornmeal mixture. Heat the remaining ingredients (except cheese) in a saucepan over medium heat until hot, then pour into the casserole. Top with spoonfuls of the reserved cornmeal mixture and sprinkle with shredded cheese. Bake at 350 degrees Fahrenheit for 25 minutes.

DORITOS CASSEROLE

2 lb Ground Beef (or Substitute Chicken)

1 pkg Taco Seasoning

1 Can Whole-Kernel Corn

1 Can Sliced Olives

1 Large Pack of Regular Doritos

2 cups Colby/Jack/Monterey Blend Cheese

Brown ground meat, add seasoning, and simmer for 5 minutes. Mix in corn, olives, and 1 cup of water for moisture. In a 9x9 casserole dish, coat the bottom with olive oil. Layer with Doritos, meat mixture, and cheese. Repeat layering, then cover with foil. Bake at 375°F for 25-30 minutes until cheese melts. Meat can be substituted with chicken.

PEPPER STEAK & RICE

2 lb thinly chopped steak

16 oz Can Tomato Sauce

8 oz Diced tomatoes
with green chili

2 tbsp Chili Powder

1 tsp Season Salt

1 tsp Black Pepper

1/2 tsp Crushed red pepper (optional)

1/2 cup Red bell pepper, sliced

1/2 cup Green bell pepper, sliced

Red Onion

3 tbsp Flour

In a mixing bowl, add chopped steak, seasoning salt, and black pepper, and mix adding. Flour toss steak in flour in a large stove top pan. Add 2tbls olive oil, stirring and browning steak. Add onion, red bell pepper, green bell pepper, chili powder, & crushed.

LASAGNA

1 whole Chicken (or 2 lb Ground Beef)

1 box Lasagna Noodles

3 lb Colby/Jack Blended Cheese

1/2 cup Feta Cheese

1/4 cup Chopped Mushrooms

1/2 cup Red Onion

1 tbsp Lawry's Seasoning Salt

1 1/2 tbsp Black Pepper

2 tbsp Chili Powder

1/2 tbsp Crushed Red Pepper

Boil chicken until done; debone, then shred with a fork in a pot. Add seasoning salt, onion, chili powder, red pepper, spaghetti sauce, diced tomatoes, spaghetti sauce, and tomato sauce; simmer for 10 minutes. Boil noodles until soft; begin the layering process in the order of noodles, mixture, seasoning, and cheese, and repeat until you reach the top pre-host oven to 375%. Bake for 45 mins.

CHICKEN TORTILLA CASEROLE (NEW)

2 double chicken breasts

1 package corn tortillas

1 lb cheese (Fiesta blend cheese)

1 can cream of mushroom soup

2 cans cream of chicken soup

1 chopped onion

1 can diced Ortega chilies (mild or spicy)

1 can sliced ripe olives

Salt and pepper to taste

Wrap chicken in foil and bake for 1 hour at 325. Debone chicken shredded—grate onion and cheese. Cut tortillas into strips—slice olives. Mix soups, olives, onion. And peppers together. Grease the baking dish: layer soup, tortillas, and chicken with cheese on top. Cover; bake at 400 ° for 1 hour. Cool and serve.

PORK MEATBALLS & WHEAT PASTA

2 lb Ground Pork

1/2 Cup Italian Breadcrumbs

1 tsp Minced Garlic

1/3 Cup Chopped Onion

1 Cup Sliced Mushrooms

1 Pack of Wheat Pasta

1 Can of Fire-Roasted Tomatoes

1 Jar of Marinara Sauce

1 tsp Chili Powder

1 tsp Oregano

1 tsp Basil

Mix ground pork, breadcrumbs, garlic, and onion in a bowl. Shape into balls and set aside. In a pan, heat olive oil and brown the meatballs. Add mushrooms, fire-roasted tomatoes, spaghetti seasoning packet, chili powder, oregano, basil, and ½ cup of water. Simmer for 25 mins. Boil six cups of water in a pot with a pinch of salt and a teaspoon of butter. Add pasta, cook until done, then drain, rinse, and serve.

WINNIE'S DRUNCKIN TURKEY (NEW)

Turkey

Poultry Seasoning

Season Salt

Black Pepper

White Wine

Brown Paper Bag

Cooking Spray

Butter

Wash turkey thoroughly. Coat with butter inside and out, season with poultry seasoning, salt, and pepper. Place a stick of butter and 1 cup of wine inside. Wrap and tie the legs. Spray a brown paper bag inside and out. Insert the turkey into the bag, clamp it closed, and bake for 2 1/2 hours. Remove from the oven, add another cup of wine, and baste by poking holes in the turkey and basting it with more wine. Return to the oven for another 1 1/2 hours or until done, depending on the turkey's size.

BASIL SUNDRIED TOMATOES, CHICKEN & PASTA, OR RICE (NEW)

Chicken

Sundried tomatoes

Mushrooms

Oregano

Onion powder

Black Pepper

Olive oil

Italian dressing

Parmesan cheese

Thin pasta or rice

In a mixing bowl, season chicken with 1 tsp olive oil, oregano, onion powder, and black pepper; add two tablespoons of oil; add chicken to hot oil and begin to sear on one side. Add mushrooms and sundried tomatoes, and a tablespoon of Italian dressing. 1/3 c water low simmer for 30 mins; serve over thin spaghetti topped with parmesan cheese.

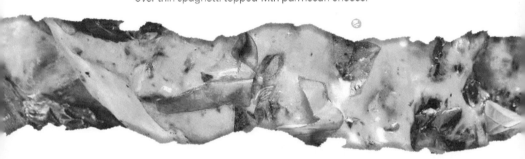

LEMON SHRIMP WITH CAPERS(NEW)

Shrimp

Olive oil

Capers

Lemons

Butter

In a frying pan, melt a stick of butter, add minced garlic, oregano, onion powder, a pinch of salt capers, simmer on low heat, lemon juice, and lemon slice, and shrimp on medium heat, constantly stirring for 3 minutes. Serve on pasta of your choice. Garnish with lemon zest and parsley.

LEMON GARLIC CHICKEN WITH CAPERS

- 1 ½ Pounds Chicken Thighs, Skin-on, Bone-in,

  One Tablespoon of Spicy Brown Mustard

  One Tablespoon Lemon Zest (1 Teaspoon Half & Half for Sauce)

- 1 ½ Teaspoons Dried Oregano

  1/2 Teaspoon Lemon Pepper

  One Tablespoon Garlic

  One Lemon Sliced

  1/3 Cup Capers

In a large skillet over medium heat, melt butter and olive oil. Sauté chicken thighs for 5-6 minutes on both sides. Set chicken aside. Add garlic cloves and cook until softened and lightly browned, about 2-3 minutes. Pour in chicken broth, scrape up any bits, and add cream, lemon juice, and half and half. Stir and bring to a slight boil. Then, add capers and return chicken to the skillet. Simmer on low for 20-2 minutes until the sauce thickens and the chicken is fully cooked.

CHICKEN PESTO CREAM CHEESE CROISSANTS WITH SUNDRIED TOMATOES

- 1 Can of Pillsbury Croissants,

  1/3 Cup Sundrinde Tomatioes

- 1 Cup of Chopped Chicken Breast

  Pesto

  Cream Cheese

Roll out croissants with a teaspoon. Spread cream cheese evenly over a croissant, spread pesto on top of cream cheese, add chicken, top with sundried tomatoes, and roll and bake at 350 degrees for 15- 20 min until golden brown

FRENCH ONION SOUP

2 lb red onions, peeled and halved, then sliced

3/4 cup butter or margarine

1 cup dry white wine

2 quarts water

6 beef bouillon cubes

8 oz Swiss or Gruyere cheese, chilled

1/2 loaf French bread

1 tsp salt

Dash of white pepper

Dash of black pepper

1 tsp Worcestershire sauce

Slice onions. Melt butter In a 4-quart. Dutch oven. Slowly cook.

TURKEY STUFFED BELL PEPPER

6 Bell Peppers

1 pound Ground Turkey

Rao Marinara Sauce

1 Packet Dry Spaghetti Seasoning

1 Onion, Chopped

Chili Powder

1 Can Fire-Roasted Chopped Tomatoes

Seasoning Salt

Onion Powder

Garlic

Black Pepper

Cauliflower Rice

Cheddar Cheese

Wash bell peppers and remove the tops for stuffing. Brown ground turkey with seasoning, onion powder, black pepper, and onions. Add marinara sauce, spaghetti seasoning, chili powder, and fire-roasted diced tomatoes. Simmer for 10 minutes. Prepare frozen cauliflower rice.Stuff bell peppers with cheddar cheese, then add rice and turkey mixture. Bake at 400°F for 50 minutes, remove, top with cheddar cheese, and bake for an additional 3-4 minutes until melted and bubbly. Serve.

SMOTHERED STUFFED PORK CHOPS

Eight Pork Chops (1 to 1 1/2 Inches Thick)

One small Onion, Finely Chopped

2 Tbsp. Butter or Margarine

314 c. Jasmine Cooked Rice

One c. (4 oz.) Shredded Cheddar
or American Cheese

1 Tsp. Worcestershire Sauce

1 1/4 Tsp. Salt

1 /8 Tsp. Black Pepper

Make a pocket in each pork chop by cutting into the center from the side, parallel to the bone and top. Cook chopped onion in butter until transparent, then add rice, cheese, Worcestershire sauce, 1/4 tsp salt, and pepper to make stuffing. Fill each pocket with about three tablespoons of the mixture. Lightly brown the chops in oil, sprinkle with one tsp salt, add a cup of water, cover, and simmer for 30-40 minutes. Makes eight servings.

STUFFED CABBAGE

2 Large Cabbage Leaves

1 lb. Ground Rurkey or Pork

1 Chopped Onion,

1 Tsp. Salt

Red Crushed Pepper

1/2 c. Cooked Rice

Egg, Slightly Beaten

One Can of Stewed Tomatoes

2 Tbsp. Garlic

3 1/4 c. Tbsp. Vegetable oil

One Reaspoon of Brown Sugar

1 Teaspoon Soy Sauce

Rice

Steam cabbage leaves for 5-7 minutes until pliant. Brown your choice of meat in a pan and add seasoning, red pepper, egg, stewed tomatoes, garlic, and brown sugar. Remove from heat. Fill cabbage leaves with the mixture and place in a greased 2-quart baking dish. Pour soy sauce over the top, sprinkle with a pinch of brown sugar. Bake covered at 350°F for 45-50 minutes, removing the cover near the end to brown the top. Adjust liquid as needed

TERIYAKI CHICKEN WITH HONEY GINGER GLAZE

1 Pack of Skinless Chicken Breast or Thighs

Honey

1 Cup Teriyaki Sauce Teriyaki Sauce

Olive Oil

Ground Ginger

Pineapple Juice

In a large mixing bowl, add chicken, season with black pepper, seasoned salt, onion salt, and olive oil, and toss, mixing well. Add half of a cup of teriyaki sauce, mix well, place in the baking pan, and place preheated at 375 degrees. Bake for 50 minutes. Remove from the oven, pour glaze over chicken, bake for 7-10 minutes until hot and sticky, remove cool, and serve.

GLAZE

In a saucepan, add half a cup of teriyaki sauce, 2 tablespoons of honey, a teaspoon of ginger, and ¼ cup of pineapple juice; bring to a boil, remove from heat, and set aside.

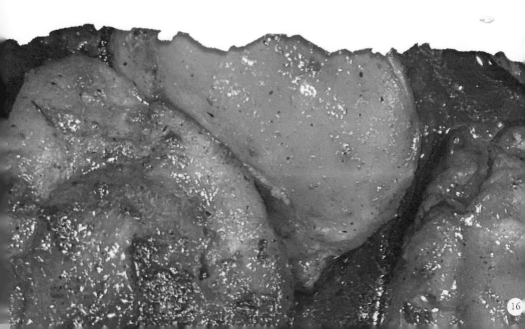

GARLIC PESTO CHICKEN

3 lb Boneless Chicken Breast or Thighs

3 Tablespoons Pesto

1 Tablespoon Garlic

Olive Oil

Garlic Salt

Pepper

Onion Powder

Mix olive oil, Pesto, Garlic, garlic salt, pepper, and onion powder; mixing well, ensure all chicken is covered and coated with the mixture, and fold into a baking dish and bake at 400 degrees for 45-60 min.

BAKED FRIED CHICKEN

Chicken

Seasoned Salt

Black Pepper

Onion Salt

Hidden Valley Ranch Seasoning

Italian Salad Dressing

Buttermilk

Olive Oil

Flour

Italian Breadcrumbs

Vegetable Spray

In a serving bowl, add chicken and Italian dressing; gracefully add seasoning salt, black pepper, onion salt, and hidden valley ranch powder; all over, add buttermilk, coating all chicken evenly. Add 1 cup of flour and 1 1/2 cup of breadcrumbs in a separate bowl. Mix well in the baking pan. Dip each piece of chicken in the flour/breadcrumb mixture and arrange it in a baking dish. Place in a preheated oven of 400 degrees bake for 50-55 minutes until golden brown oven may vary

SPIRAL BOURBON GLAZED HAM

1 Spiral Ham	11/2 Cup Bourbon
1 Can Sliced Pineapple	Brown Sugar

Spicey Brown Mustard

Place spiral ham in a roasting pan. Take a pinch of brown sugar and sprinkle between each slice of ham, followed by pouring half cup of bourbon over the ham, allowing to drip between slices. Place cover and place in preheated oven to 375 degrees for 45 minutes, then lowering oven to 325 degrees remain cooking for additional 40 minutes remove from oven place pineapple rings all over ham then pour hot prepared glaze over ham place back in oven cook uncovered for 20 minutes remove and serve.

BOURBON GLAZE

½ C Bourbon

½ C Dark Brown Sugar

¼ C Pineapple Juice

1 Teaspoon Spicy Brown Sugar

In saucepan pour bourbon, pineapple juice, brown sugar, spicy mustard simmer brings to boil. Remove from heat.

CATFISH NUGGETS

3 Pounds of Catfish

Three Eggs

2 ½ Cups Yellow Cornmeal

Old bay Seasoning

1 Tsp Onion Powder

Red Chili Flakes

One Tbs Black Pepper

2-3 C Oil

In a mixing bowl, dice your fish into nuggets. Cut one piece of fish into 3-4 pieces. Add old bay seasoning, red chili flakes, black pepper, and onion powder, and mix well in a small bowl. Beat three eggs, pour over fish, and mix well in a separate mixing bowl; add corn meal, a teaspoon of old bay seasoning, and red chili flakes. Stir well.

Prepare a frying pan or deep fryer, your choice. Fill with oil. Ensure your oil is piping hot test by dropping a pinch of cornmeal in the oil. If it begins to fry, you know it's time taking a little at a time. Take your fish dip in corn meal, assuring it's completely covered, then place it in hot oil. Once golden on both sides, remove from oil and repeat until all fish is done and ready to serve.

DESSERT

PIE CRUST

2 Cups Flour

One Stick of Softened
Butter or Butter Crisco

1 Tsp Milk

2 Tsp Water

1/3 Cup Sugar

Mixing bowl, add flour and butter, milk, water, and sugar, and begin kneading until
you have a ball. Place on a cutting board and use a rolling pin with a butterknife to
cut the dough in a moon shape. Take tables of apricot mixture spread inside the
crust... Fold over, pinch around edges, lightly dust lightly with flour, place in the frying
pan of hot oil on low heat as crust gets golden brown, flip over brown other side, and
remove. Serve with vanilla ice cream.

WINNIE'S FUDGE

1 ½ lb semi-sweet chocolate

1/8 lb butter or margarine

¼ tsp salt

1 tsp vanilla

2-3 cups of chopped nuts, optional

4 ½ c sugar

One can evaporate milk

Combine sugar and milk. Cook over low heat until it comes to a boil.
Approx. 5-6 minutes. Remove from stove and add remainder of
ingredients. Blend and pour into the baking dish —place in
freezer for 1 hour. Remove and cut into squares serve.

LEE'S APPLE PIE

3/4 c. sugar

1/4 c. all-purpose flour 1/2 tsp. nutmeg

1/2 tsp. cinnamon dash of salt

Six c. thinly sliced apples (about five medium)

2 Tbsp. Butter or margarine

1 (9-inch) pie shell

Preheat oven to 425°F. Mix sugar, flour, nutmeg, cinnamon, and salt with apples. Pour into pie crust, dot with butter, and cover with the top crust.Cut slits in the crust, seal, and flute the edges. Cover the crust edge with foil strips to prevent excessive browning. Remove foil for the last 15 minutes of baking.Bake for 40-50 minutes until the crust is browned and juices bubble through the slits. Enjoy!

MAMA'S OLD FASHIONED SWEET POTATO PIE

21/2 c. cooked mashed sweet potatoes

1/2 c. butter or margarine

Two c. sugar

1 Tbsp. flour

1/2 tsp. salt

1/2 tsp. ground nutmeg or allspice

/2 tsp. ground ginger 1/2 tsp. cinnamon

Four eggs, beaten

One can evaporate milk

2 (9-inch) pie shells

Preheat oven to 425 °. Combine potatoes and butt. Er, you are mixing well until blended. Add combined sug flour, and spices; mix well. Blend in eggs and milk. Pour into unbaked pie shells. Bake for 10 minutes on top o middle of the oven on 350 for 50 to 60 min or until the toothpick in the center of the pie comes out clean.

TRIPPLE CHOCOLATE POUND CAKE

2 sticks margarine 1/2 c. shortening three c. sugar

Five eggs Three c. flour

/4 tsp. salt

1/2 tsp. baking powder 1/2 c. cocoa

1 1/2 c. milk

1 tsp. vanilla

8oz pack chocolate fudge pudding mix

12 cups dark chocolate chips

Cream margarine, shortening, and sugar together; add eggs. Sift dry ingredients together; add to the creamed mixture. Add chocolate chips a little at a time by alternating with milk. Add vanilla. Bake at 325•. for 1 hour or 300 ° for 1 1/4 hours.

LEE MARY'S TEA CAKES

Two c. sugar

2 tsp. baking powder

One c. shortening, butter, or margarine

Two eggs

One c. buttermilk

2 Tbsp. vanilla

1 1/2 tsp. Nutmeg

1 tsp. baking soda 5 to 6 c. flour

Cream together sugar, baking powder, shortening, and eggs. Add buttermilk, vanilla, nutmeg, baking soda, and flour. Mix them all together. Roll out and cut with a biscuit cutter. Makes about 30 cookies.

SPICY ZUCCHINI BREAD

Three c. unsifted flour

1 tsp. baking soda

1/4 tsp. baking powder

1 tsp. salt

2 1/2 tsp. Cinnamon

1/4 tsp. nutmeg

3eggs

Two c. sugar

One c. salad oil

Two c. raw zucchini (unpeeled), grated

3 tsp. vanilla

One c. chopped nuts and handful of raisins

Combine flour, baking soda, baking powder, salt, and spices. Set aside. In a large bowl, lightly beat eggs. Stir in sugar and oil until well mixed. Add the flour mixture, stirring just enough to blend. Mix in zucchini, vanilla, nuts, and raisins. Pour the batter into two greased 9 x 5 x 3-inch loaf pans. Bake in a preheated 350°F oven for 50-60 minutes until done. Cool on a rack for 5 minutes before removing from pans. Makes two loaves.

MAMA'S PECAN PIE

Three eggs

2/3 c. sugar

One c. white Karo syrup

1/4 c. butter or margarine, melted

/4 tsp. salt

1 tsp. Vanilla flavor one c. chopped pecan

Beat eggs; add sugar, syrup, butter, salt, and vanilla flavor. Blend well; add pecans. Bake at 400" for 10 minutes. Bake at 350 ° for 30 to 40 minutes.

BLUEBERRY CHOCOLATE CHIP PEANUT BUTTER NO BAKED COOKIES

/2 c. Peanut Butter

1/4 c. Butter

One c. Sugar

½ c Dried Cranberries

½ c Dark Chocolate Chips

Cream peanut butter and sugar together. Adding cranberries. And chocolate chip mixture. Roll into balls the size of walnuts. Roll in powdered sugar and press with a fork to shape the cookie. Bake at 325 for 12 min.

GERMAN CHOCOLATE CAKE

1/4oz Pkg Bakers German Sweet Chocolate

½ c Boiling Water

1c. Butte or Margring

2 c Sugar

Four Eggs Yolks

1 Tsp Vanilla

Two ¼ c Sifted all-Purpose Flour

1 Tsp. Baking Soda

½ Tsp. Salt

1 c Buttermilk

Four Egg Whites Stiffly Beaten

Melt chocolate in boiling water and cool. Cream butter and sugar until fluffy. Add yolks one at a time, beating well after each. Blend in vanilla and chocolate. Sift flour with soda and salt. Add buttermilk to the chocolate mixture alternately, beating until smooth. Fold in beaten egg whites. Pour into three 9-inch layer pans lined with paper on the bottoms. Bake at 350°F for 30-35 minutes, then cool. Frost the tops only. Whole cake assembly is optional.

COCONUT-PECAN FROSTING

One c. Evaporated Milk

One c. Sugar

Three Slightly beaten Egg Yolks

1/2 c. Butter or Margarine

1 tsp. vanilla

1 1/3 c. Baker's Angel Flake Coconut

One c. chopped pecans

Combine milk, sugar, egg yolks, butter, margarine, and vanilla. Cook and stir over medium heat until thickened about 12 minutes. Add coconut and pecans. Cool until thick enough to spread, beating occasionally. Makes 2 1/2 cups.

SOCK IT TO ME CAKE

1 Package Duncan Hines Cake Mix

1 Cup (8 oz.) Dairy Sour Cream

1 1/2 Cups Oil

1/4 Cup Sugar

1/4 Cup Water

4 Eggs

Filling:

1 Cup Chopped Pecans

2 Tablespoons Brown Sugar

2 Teaspoons Cinnamon

Preheat the oven to 375°F. In a large bowl, mix together the cake mix, sour cream, oil, sugar, water, and eggs. Beat at high speed for 2 minutes. Pour 2/3 of the batter into a greased and floured 10-inch pan. In a separate bowl, combine the chopped pecans, brown sugar, and cinnamon for the filling. Sprinkle the filling mixture evenly over the batter in the pan. Pour the remaining batter over the filling. Bake in the preheated oven. It will serve 12 to 16 people.

BANANA PUDDING

1/2 cup granulated sugar

3 tablespoons all-purpose flour

1/2 teaspoon vanilla extract

A dash of salt

5 to 6 medium fully ripe bananas, sliced

4 eggs

2 3/4 cups milk

Nilla wafers

Combine 1/2 cup sugar, flour, and salt in a double boiler. Mix in one whole egg and three egg yolks. Stir in milk. Cook covered over boiling water, stirring constantly until thickened. Remove from heat; add vanilla. Spread a small amount on the bottom of a 1 1/2-quart casserole dish; cover with a layer of Nilla wafers. Top with layers of sliced bananas. Pour about 1/3 cup of custard over the bananas. Layer wafers, bananas, and custard to make three layers of each, ending with custard. Beat the remaining three egg whites until stiff but not dry; gradually add the remaining 1/4 cup sugar and beat until the mixture forms stiff peaks. Pile the beaten egg whites on top of the pudding, covering the entire surface. Bake in a preheated hot oven (425°F) for 5 minutes or until delicately browned. Serve warm or chilled. Makes eight servings.

CHEESECAKE

1 small box lemon Jello

1/2 cup sugar

1 (20 oz.) can crushed pineapple

1 large container of Cool Whip

1 large cream cheese block

1 teaspoon vanilla extract

1 graham cracker crust (8-inch)

Make lemon Jello using pineapple juice and water. Let it cool. Cream sugar and cream cheese together. Mix in cooled Jello, crushed pineapple, and vanilla. Gently fold in Cool Whip. Pour into an 8-inch graham cracker crust. Chill overnight.

7-UP CAKE

1 1/2 c. butter

Five eggs

3 C-sugar

2 Tbsp. lemon flavor

2 ½ c flour

3/4c. 7-Up

Cream butter and sugar together; add eggs, one at a time, and beat well after each addition. Add flour, small amount a at a time. Add 7-Up, then fold in lemon flavor. Bake 350 for 1 hour and 10 mins. Don't open the oven while the cake is baking. Let cool for five min, flip, and serve.

PEANUT BRITTLE

2c. white sugar

3c.raw peanuts

3/4 c. white Karo syrup

One heaping Tbsp. soda

1/2 stick butter or margarine

Mix sugar, syrup, and butter in a large, heavy pan. Heat until the sugar is melted and comes to a good boil. Add peanuts and cook 10 to 12 minutes until it is golden brown. Stir to keep from sticking. Remove from fire; add soda. Stir frequently and pour into a well-greased cookie sheet. Spread thinly

TRIPPLE CHOCOLATE SUGAR-FREE CUPCAKES

1 BOX Pillsbury Sugar-free Cake Mix.

One box of Sugar-free Chocolate Pudding

One jar of Pillsbury sugar-free Chocolate Fudge Frosting

½ Cup of Dark Chocolate Chips

Mix cake mix following directions. Fold in chocolate pudding and mix well, adding chocolate chips. Bake at 325 degrees for 25 mins.

APRICOT FRIED PIES

1 Pound of Dried Apricots

One Stick of Butter

Tbls of Cornstarch

1 Tsp Allspice

n a saucepan on the top stove, add ¼ cup of water and bring to a boil. Add dried apricots and bring to a simmer; add remaining ingredients and bring to a bubbly simmer as it thickens. Remove from heat and set aside.

PEANUT BUTTER CRANBERRY COOKIES

One c. natural peanut butter

One egg

½ cup sugar or sugar substitute

¼ cup of dried cranberry

Add peanut butter, sugar, and egg in a mixing bowl and fold in cranberry mix very well. Preheat oven to 325 degrees. Using a small scoop, create a mixture, roll it into a ball, place it on a nonstick cookie sheet, take a fork, dip it into the water, press each ball into a cookie shape, and bake for 10-12 minutes. Cool and serve

BAILEYS, CINNAMON FRENCH CUSTARD TOAST

One loaf of French bread sliced

4Tbsp. margarine

1 cup half & half

One can of Eagle Brand milk

½ cup Bailey Irish cream

Large tablespoon sugar

Large tablespoon of brown sugar

Two tablespoons of cinnamon

spread bread slices in a baking dish, then sprinkle on sugar, brown sugar, and butter. Use a spoon to mix sugar and butter. Next, add half & half, eagle brand milk, mixing well, sprinkle with cinnamon, pour Bailey Irish cream, place in preheated oven at 365 degrees, and bake for 35- 40 min.

LEMON PINEAPPLE UP-SIDE DOWN CUPCAKE

One Box of Pillsbury Sugar-free Yellow Cake Mix.

½ C Crushed Pineapple

One Pack of Free Lemon Pudding Mix

One Teaspoon of Plain Yogurt

Three Eggs

1/3 C oil

1 c Water

Mixing bowl, add box cake mix three eggs, oil, and water, mix very well, and fold in pineapple. Mix well. Add yogurt and continue mixing. Spray cupcake tins with nonstick baking oil. Fill tins and place in a preheated oven of 325 degrees. Bake for 20-25 min. Oven may vary.

LEMON CREAM CHEESE PINEAPPLE FROSTING

Pillsbury Sugar-free Vanilla Frosting

One Tablespoon of Lemon Juice

¼ C Crushed Pineapple

¼ C Cream Cheese

Mixing bowl, add frosting, lemon juice, crushed pineapple, and cream cheese. Mix well and chill for 1 hour. Frost semi-warm cupcakes and serve.

BETTER THAN SEX CHOCOLATE PIE(NEW)

Two eggs, separated.

1 1/2 c. water

3/4 c. sugar

/3 c. grated bitter

chocolate or cocoa

1/8 tsp. salt

1 Tbsp. butter

1 tsp. vanilla flavor

5 Tbsp. flour

One stick of cream cheese

Beat egg yolks lightly and add water. Blend dry ingredients into liquid mixtures. Place in double boiler; cook until thick, stirring constantly. Remove from heat; add vanilla and butter. Let cool for 45 min. Begin to layer with chocolate mixture cream refrigerate 1 hour serve.

GINGERBREAD(NEW)

/2 c. sugar

One egg

1/2 c. shortening

One c. molasses

1/2 c. flour

2 Tbsp. ginger

1 1/2 tsp. baking soda

One c. hot water

1/3 c. Dr. Pepper's room temp

Cream sugar and shortening; add egg. Add 1 cup of molasses. Add flour, ginger, and soda to the shortening mixture. Add hot water and Dr Pepper and mix well. Bake in a greased and floured pan for 25

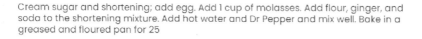

SIDES

SPICY MASHED POTATOES

5 lb potatoes, cooked and mashed

2 cups sour cream

2 (3 oz.) packages cream cheese

Salt and pepper to taste

2 tablespoons Hidden Valley Ranch spicy seasoning

1 1/2 sticks butter

Combine all ingredients, mix well, and serve.

BLACK-EYED PEAS AND SMOKED TURKEY

1 lb dried black-eyed peas

2 lb smoked turkey

2 chopped onions

2 stalks of celery, chopped

1 small bay leaf

1 clove garlic

1 pod of hot red pepper

1 small can of tomato sauce

2 tbsp chili sauce

Boiling water

Wash the peas and set aside. Bring onion and celery, garlic, and pepper to a boil. Add black-eyed peas and smoked turkey, adding liquid as needed. Cover; simmer until tender, about 3 hours. Serves 6 to 8.

GARLIC GREEN BEANS WITH BACON

1 lb Fresh Green Beans

4 Slices Bacon

1 tablespoon Garlic

1/4 cup Chopped Onion

1 tablespoon Season Salt

1 tablespoon Black Pepper

Large skillet for safe sift but y bacon to crisp do not drain add garlic, onion, stirring consistently add green beans, salt & pepper, cook on lower heat covered stir until green beans are soft but still has a crunch.

NANA'S SOUTHERN MAC & CHEESE

2 Boxes Elbow Macaroni Moodles

1 lb Cheddar Cheese

2/3 Cup Monterey Jack Cheese

1/2 Cup Pepper Jack Cheese

1 Cup Milk

1 Tablespoon Season Salt

1 Tablespoon Black Pepper

1 Teaspoon Garlic

2 Eggs

Boil noodles, rinse, and drain. In a blender, mix milk, seasoning salt, black pepper, garlic, and two eggs until well blended. Combine all three cheeses in a bowl and set aside. Butter a large casserole dish. Start layering: cheese, pasta, repeat until the final layer is cheese. Pour the blended mixture evenly over the dish. Bake at 350°F for 45-50 minutes

PASTA SALAD

2 Boxes of Tricolor Pasta Noodles

1 Bottle of Kraft Tuscan Italian Dressing

1 Cup Dried Tomatoes

8 oz. Can Sliced Olives

1 Package Shredded Parmesan Cheese

1/3 Cup Finely Chopped Red Onion

One 12 oz Package Real Bacon Bits

1/2 Tablespoon Seasoned Salt

1/2 Tablespoon Black Pepper

Boil and drain noodles. Combine pasta, sun-dried tomatoes, olives, onions, Parisian cheese, bacon bits, seasoned salt, and pepper in a bowl. Toss well. Add dressing in small amounts, mixing thoroughly. Refrigerate for 1 hour before serving. Toss steak in flour. Brown steak in a pan with olive oil. Add onion, red and green bell pepper, chili powder, and crushed black pepper. Stir and cook until done.

NANA'S OKRA AND TOMATOES

1 1 /2 c. Cut Okra.

1 1/2 c. Cut up Tomatoes.

1/4c Finely Chopped Bell pepper

1/2 Medium Onion, Cut up Salt and Pepper, to Taste.

Sauté okra and onion together; add tomatoes. H using fresh tomatoes, add 1/4 cup of tomato sauce. Cook for about 15 minutes.

CORNBREAD DRESSING

4 Boxes Jiffy Cornbread Mix

2 Onions, Chopped

2 Green Bell Peppers, Chopped

1 Stalk of Celery, Chopped

3 Sticks of Unsalted Butter

2 Boxes of Ms. Cubbins
Cornbread Dressing Mix

4 cans of chicken broth

1 Cup Sugar

Prepare the cornbread boxes, add 1 cup of sugar, bake, and set aside. Prepare onions, bell peppers, and celery, and cook in a crockpot for 12 hours. In a large mixing bowl, crumble cornbread, add chicken broth, fold in onion mixture, and reaming broth. Pour into a baking pan and bake at 350 for an hour.

BAKED BEANS

2 Large Cans of Baked Beans

1 Cup Brown Sugar

12 oz Can Crushed Pineapple

1/2 Cup Barbecue (BBQ) Sauce

1/2 Cup chopped green onions

1/2 Cup Real Bacon Bits

Mix beans, folding in brown sugar, crushed pineapple, barb que sauce, in a large baking dish, generously top with baking bits and green onions, and bake at 375 degrees 45-60mmins until golden brown and bubbly on top.

ZUCCHINI, CARROTS, & BROCCOLI STEAMED VEGETABLES SALT

1/2 lb Baby Peeled Carrots

1/2 lb Broccoli

1/2 lb Zucchini

5 Tablespoons Butter

5 Tablespoons Water

1 Tablespoon Seasoning (Your Choice)

1 Tablespoon Black Pepper (Adjust to Taste)

Bring Water and butter to a slight boil. Add zucchini, carrots, broccoli, season salt & and pepper, and cover simmer for 5-8 minutes until tender. Toss season to taste to serve.

MAMA'S CANDIED YAMS

4 Sticks of Butter or Margarine

1 Cup Sugar

Pinch of Salt

3 Medium Yams

1 Tablespoon Nutmeg

1 Teaspoon Vanilla Flavor

1 1/2 Cups Water

Peel and cut yams in quarters. Sprinkle sugar, nutmeg, and butter. Cover and simmer over medium heat until liquid forms a syrup. Remove from heat and serve.

POTATO SALAD

6 Potatoes

1 teaspoon Seasoned Salt

1/4 cup Sweet Pickle Relish

1/4 cup Chopped Red Onion

3/4 Eggs

Pinch of Salt and Pepper

1/2 cup Sandwich Spread (e.g., Kraft)

1 teaspoon Brown Mustard

Boil potatoes and drain. Add pickle, relish onions, eggs, sugar, salt, and pepper to taste. Sandwich spread, mustard, cover, refrigerate for 2 hours, sprinkle paprika on top, and serve.

TACO SALAD

1 Head Lettuce

1 pound Ground Beef

Medium Tomatoes, Cubed

1/2 Cup Jack Cheese, Diced

1/2 Cup Chopped Green Onions

1 Avocado, Sliced (Optional)

1 Tablespoon Olive Oil

1 Quart Dressing of Your Choice

1 Packet Taco Seasoning

1 Cup Black Olives, sliced

1 Cup Garlic (quantity might be too much; you can adjust to taste)

Wash Lettuce and core, and break into shredded pieces. Refrigera prepared ground beef in a 10-inch skillet with oil and garlic. sauté until brown. Drain fat, add taco seasoning, and set aside until coo Mix all ingredients except Dressing. Add Dressing when ready to se

ITALIAN CHOPPED SALAD

1/2 head Iceberg Lettuce

1/2 head Romaine Lettuce

Two Ripe Tomatoes

One Bunch of Radishes, sliced

4 to 6 Green Onions

1/2 pound Italian Salami

1/2 pound Provolone Cheese

Oil and Vinegar (for dressing)

Finely chop all the ingredients, except the radishes. Add radish slices. Toss with oil and vinegar or Italian. Dressing.

SPINACH SALAD

Two Bunches of Fresh Spinach, Washed Thoroughly.

Three GreenOnions, Chopped.

One Avocado, Peeled and Cubed.

Four Hard-Cooked Eggs, Mashed.

Seasoned Pepper (to Taste).

Eight Strips of Bacon, Cooked and Crumbled.

1 Cup Seasoned Croutons.

1 Cup Sliced Fresh Mushrooms (Optional).

Oil and Vinegar Dressing (or Dressing of your choice).

Toss all vegetables together and add. Dressing. Spring kale mashed eggs and crumbled bacon over the top. Toss again lightly. Serve on individual salad plates or in a large salad bowl. Add croutons. Makes 24 servings.

GREEK SALAD

One head of romaine lettuce

1 Green pepper

1 Cucumber

1/2 sliced red onion

Sliced cherry tomatoes

Kalamata olives

Feta cheese

Dried crisp onions

Toss and serve with balsamic Dressing.

STRAWBERRY SPINACH CHICKEN SALAD

Spinach Salad

Spring Mix Salad

Strawberries

Chicken breast

Cherry tomatoes

Minced garlic

Olive Oil

Onion

Mushrooms

Feta Cheese

Balsamic dressing or dressing of your choice

Add spinach, spring mix, cherry tomatoes, strawberries, and mushrooms in a mixing bowl. Set it aside. In a frying pan, 1 tbs olive oil heat, add minced garlic, onion, and thinly sliced chicken until chicken is cooked through. Adding chicken to the salad mixture, toss with feta cheese, and serve with the dressing of choice.

GARLIC ROASTED POTATOES

5 Red Potatoes

1 ½ Tablespoons Olive Oil

2 Tablespoon Garlic

1 Teaspoon Onion Salt

1 Dry Pack Onion Soup Mix

Wash potatoes dice into cubes, put in a large mixing bowl, add ingredients, olive oil, garlic, onion salt, onion soup mix, mixing all ingredients very well spread out on a non-stick cooking sheet cover, and bake in preheated oven 375 degrees for 40 minutes remove covering and continue to bake for ten additional minutes.

SOUTHERN APPLE CIDER VINEGAR CUCUMBER TOMATO & ONIONS

3Large   Cucumbers

Sliced Tomatoes

1/2c   Sliced Red Onion

2c Apple Cider Vinegar

3tlbs Sugar

1tbs Black Pepper

Add Sliced Cumbers, Sliced Tomatoes, Red Onion, and black pepper in a mixing bowl. Toss, add Apple Cider Vinegar and sugar, stir, and refrigerate. Chill for two hours and serve.

COLLARD GREENS

Bunches of Greens

Smoked Turkey

Ham hocks

Garlic

Onion Powder

Teaspoon Oil

Two Chopped Yellow Onions

Chopped of Hot Peppers of Your Choice

½ C Broth

In a large pot, add four cups of water, black pepper, onion powder, garlic oil, and smoked turkey, and bring to a boil. Add greens and ham hocks. Lower heat and simmer, stirring periodically until tender to your liking and taste.

ABOUT THE AUTHOR

From Winnie's kitchen to your table, cooking with love for me is creating and mixing ingredients and flavors to create a mouthwatering dish. It is so unique and satisfying to watch your family take that first bite; the expression is love!

My love for cooking comes from my mother, grandmother, and Aunt. I can remember as a little girl pulling up a chair in the kitchen as my mom, grandma, and aunt would prepare meals, running my fingers through dough for dinner rolls or pie crust, and much more every step of cooking from then to now is all about love and family. Of course, they never used recipes. All dishes were made from scratch and tasted.

As a single mom working daily and creating dinners, I have designed my recipes to be time-saving and flavorful. As much as I enjoy cooking and creating new dishes, appetizers, and desserts, I hope you enjoy creating my dishes for your family and friends.

My cookbook is dedicated to the loves of my life, Ishala & kahlas, and my entire family. May you always enjoy creating the dishes we have shared at our table of love.

9798869117267